How the Internet Is Changing Society

Carla Mooney

ReferencePoint
Press®

San Diego, CA

Science, Technology, and Society

ReferencePoint
Press®

About the Author

Carla Mooney is the author of many books for young
adults and children. She lives in Pittsburgh, Pennsylvania,
with her husband and three children.

© 2016 ReferencePoint Press, Inc.
Printed in the United States

For more information, contact:
ReferencePoint Press, Inc.
PO Box 27779
San Diego, CA 92198
www.ReferencePointPress.com

Picture Credits:
Cover: Thinkstock Images; Maury Aaseng: 19, 23; © Jim Bennett/Corbis: 68; Bloomua/Shutterstock.com:
36; © Brian Cahn/ZUMA Press/Corbis: 14; © Corbis: 13; Depositphotos : 6 (top), 7, 9, 39, 62; © Marcus
Golejewski/Geisler-Fotopr/dpa/Corbis: 56; © Kurt Krieger/Corbis: 29; Ekaterina Minaeva/Shutterstock.com:
43; © Steven Senne/AP/Corbis: 64; © Scott Stulberg/Corbis: 25; Thinkstock Images: 1, 6 (bottom); © Peter
Turnley/Corbis: 52; © xPACIFICA/Corbis: 49

LIBRARY OF CONGRESS CATALOGING-IN-PUBLICATION DATA

Mooney, Carla, 1970-
 How the Internet is changing society / by Carla Mooney.
    pages cm. -- (Science, technology, and society series)
 Includes bibliographical references and index.
 ISBN-13: 978-1-60152-900-8 (hardback)
 ISBN-10: 1-60152-900-7 (hardback)
 1. Internet--Social aspects--Juvenile literature. 2. Information society--Juvenile literature.
I. Title.
 HM851.M625 2016
 302.23'1--dc23
                                                                        2015005635

Contents

"Science and technology have had a major impact on society, and their impact is growing. By drastically changing our means of communication, the way we work, our housing, clothes, and food, our methods of transportation, and, indeed, even the length and quality of life itself, science has generated changes in the moral values and basic philosophies of mankind.

"Beginning with the plow, science has changed how we live and what we believe. By making life easier, science has given man the chance to pursue societal concerns such as ethics, aesthetics, education, and justice; to create cultures; and to improve human conditions. But it has also placed us in the unique position of being able to destroy ourselves."

— Donald P. Hearth, former director of the
NASA Langley Research Center, 1985.

Donald P. Hearth wrote these words in 1985. They appear in the foreword of a publication titled *The Impact of Science on Society*, a collection of speeches given during a public lecture series of the same name. Although Hearth's words were written about three decades ago, they are as true today as when they first appeared on the page.

Advances in science and technology undeniably bring about societal change. Gene therapy, for instance, has the potential to revolutionize medicine and the treatment of debilitating illnesses such as sickle-cell anemia and Parkinson's disease. Medical experts say gene therapy might also be used to treat conditions ranging from obesity to depression and someday, perhaps, even to help extend human life spans.

Although gene therapy offers great hope and promise, it also carries significant risks. The 1999 death of an eighteen-year-old patient taking part in a gene therapy clinical trial in the United States provided a painful reminder of the need for strict safeguards and monitoring. Other risks may be less tangible for the time being, but they are no less serious. The idea of changing the genetic instructions for human beings can be construed in some instances as arrogant, immoral, and dangerous. The possibility of making such changes raises questions of who should decide which traits are normal and desirable and which are to be considered unhealthy. It raises questions about the enhancement of the intellectual and athletic capabilities of individuals and about the potential for discrimination against those judged to be in possession of less desirable or faulty genes.

ReferencePoint's *Science, Technology, and Society* series examines scientific and technological advances in the context of their impact on society. Topics covered in the series include gene therapy, the Internet, renewable energy, robotics, and mobile devices. Each book explores how and why this science or technology came about; how it has influenced or shaped daily life and culture; efforts to guide or control the technology through laws and policies; and what the next generation of this technology might look like. Included in the chapters are focus questions aimed at eliciting conversation and debate. Also included are key words and terms and their meanings in the context of the topics covered. Fully documented quotes enliven the narrative and add to the usefulness of the series as a tool for student researchers.

The study of science, technology, and society—sometimes referred to as STS—has gained significant ground in recent years. Top universities, including Stanford and UC Berkeley in California and MIT and Harvard in Massachusetts, are among the many that offer majors or specialized programs devoted to the study of science, technology, and society. The National Science Foundation, an independent federal agency created by Congress in 1950, even has a program that funds research and education specifically on this topic. For secondary students interested in this field, or for those who are merely curious or just trying to fulfill an assignment, ReferencePoint's new series can provide a useful and accessible starting point.

1969
The first message on the ARPAnet is sent.

1958
The United States government creates the Advanced Research Projects Agency (ARPA) to improve the country's technological abilities.

1974
The term *Internet* is first used by Vinton Cerf, one of the developers of TCP/IP protocol.

1993
The National Center for Supercomputing Applications (NCSA) releases Mosaic 1.0, the first web browser to become popular with the general public.

1991
Tim Berners-Lee's World Wide Web is introduced.

1967
Design begins on ARPAnet, which would become an early version of the Internet.

1994
Yahoo! is created by Stanford University graduate students Jerry Yang and David Filo.

1973
Development begins on TCP/IP protocol that will allow diverse computer networks to interconnect and communicate with each other.

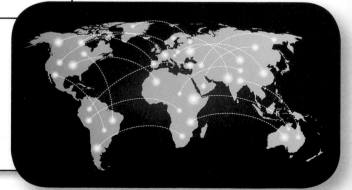

1995
Amazon.com, which describes itself as "Earth's Biggest Bookstore," launches.

1998
The first blogs appear.

2006
Twitter launches.

2011
Young Egyptians use the hashtags #Egypt and #Jan25 on Twitter to spread the word about the Egyptian Revolution; the government responds by shutting down the Internet in the nation.

2002
Social networking site Friendster.com begins.

2004
Harvard student Mark Zuckerberg starts a social network called Facebook.

2014
Seventy-one percent of Americans own a smartphone with mobile Internet access.

2005
Broadband Internet connections surpass dial-up connections.

2010
Social photo-sharing sites Pinterest and Instagram become available to users.

1996
E-mail surpasses postal mail in the United States.

A Transformative Technology

In the years since its introduction, the Internet has emerged as one of the most transformative technologies in human history. Thanks to the Internet, billions of people around the world have access to more information than ever before. They communicate with each other across vast distances almost instantaneously and have an outlet to share content with friends and strangers around the globe. And increasingly, users are not tethered to desktop computers to access the Internet. Instead they go online with mobile devices that they carry everywhere.

Even simple tasks such as going to the movies have been transformed by the Internet. Today's moviegoers can go online to watch movie trailers and read critic reviews to help them decide which film to see. Then they can search theaters and movie times online. They can even skip theater lines and purchase their movie tickets online. Months after they see the film, movie fans can download a movie's digital copy to a home computer or tablet to watch again. Eric Schmidt, the executive chairman of Google, and Jared Cohen, the founder and director of Google Ideas, believe the Internet has significantly impacted societies worldwide. "Mass adoption of the Internet is driving one of the most exciting social, cultural, and political transformations in history, and unlike earlier periods of change, this time the effects are fully global,"[1] write Schmidt and Cohen in their book *The New Digital Age*.

A Multifaceted Tool

Across society the Internet is a multifaceted tool that has become an integral part of daily life. For many people the

Internet has become a one-stop shop for information. Using a search engine and a few mouse clicks or fingertip movements, users can find anything from news to recipes to maps. They can get turn-by-turn directions, information about a medical procedure, or even the weather forecast for the coming week.

transformative

Causing or able to cause a change.

In addition, the Internet has become an indispensable communication tool. Online, users can connect with friends, family, and even people they have never met before in a matter of seconds. They can send e-mails and instant messages. They can post statuses and comments on social media sites and blogs. They can even make Internet-based phone calls using Voice over Internet Protocol (VoIP) services or video conference calls via Skype.

The Internet has also changed the way people access media and entertainment. From the comfort of their homes users go to the Internet to read online newspapers and magazines. They watch episodes of their favorite television shows whenever they want on computers and Internet-connected devices. From these

The Internet has transformed the experience of moviegoing. Not only can viewers read reviews, watch movie trailers, and purchase tickets online, they can also access films to watch on a home computer or portable device.

devices they can watch music videos, listen to streaming music, or download a music album. Many radio stations around the world broadcast online along with online-only radio stations. Video game enthusiasts can play against others who live across town, across the country, or in other parts of the world.

The Internet has changed how people shop, save, and invest their money. Online banking allows people to pay bills, transfer money between accounts, and make investments from their homes. The shopping experience has also expanded beyond geographical borders with shoppers no longer limited to the items carried by their local stores. With the Internet they can shop and purchase items from anywhere in the world and have them shipped directly to their front door.

> **interactive**
>
> Having a two-way transfer of information.

In recent years the Internet has undergone another transformation, becoming a more interactive technology. In the early years of the Internet users simply read the information they found online. Today users shape the web by adding their own content to it, from articles and blogs to videos and photographs.

Just the Beginning

In the short time since its introduction the Internet has changed society in many ways, from the way people find information to how they communicate and access media. Because the Internet and how it is used is constantly changing, many people believe that the Internet's impact has just begun, with many more changes to come. "And yet we are still in the early stages of the transformations the Internet will unleash and the opportunities it will foster. Many more technological innovations and enabling capabilities . . . are likely to emerge, while the ability to connect many more people and things and engage them more deeply will continue to expand exponentially,"[2] write global business and economics experts James Manyika and Charles Roxburgh from management consulting firm McKinsey & Company. As the Internet continues to evolve, the technologies and devices of the future will give society the ability to use the Internet in new and exciting ways.

Chapter One

Connecting Computers Worldwide

"Cyberspace is now an unavoidable reality that wraps our planet in a complex information and communications skin."

—Ronald J. Deibert, professor of political science and director of the Canada Centre for Global Security Studies and the Citizen Lab at the Munk School of Global Affairs, University of Toronto.

Ronald J. Deibert, *Black Code: Surveillance, Privacy and the Dark Side of the Internet*. Toronto, ON: McClelland & Stewart, 2013, p. 2.

———————————————————

Even though the Internet has existed for only a short time, it is hard to imagine life without it. The Internet connects billions of people and devices around the world through a global system of interconnected computer networks. Sometimes the Internet is described as an enormous spiderweb that connects everything from computers and tablets to GPS devices and cell phones. Thirty years ago, however, it did not exist. The Internet was just an idea shared by a few scientists. So how did it all start?

> **network**
>
> A system of connected computers and related devices used to send or receive information.

Birth of the Internet

Unlike inventions such as the light bulb and telephone, the Internet does not have a single inventor. Instead, it evolved over time through the efforts of many people. In 1958 President Dwight D. Eisenhower created the Advanced Research Projects Agency (ARPA). The Soviet Union had just launched Sputnik, the world's first man-made satellite, into orbit in 1957, and many people feared that the United

States was falling behind its Soviet rival technologically. Eisenhower wanted ARPA to give the United States a technological advantage over other countries, including the Soviet Union.

One of ARPA's goals was to improve the country's computer science capabilities. In the late 1950s and early 1960s computers were huge machines that filled an entire room. Many computers read magnetic tape or punch cards. Compared to modern machines, the computers of this era had significantly less processing power. They were used as enormous calculators, not as communication tools. Additionally, each computer operated on a stand-alone basis, and there were no computer networks. If two computers were running on different operating systems, they could not communicate with each other.

At the time, the United States relied on a network of telephone lines to communicate quickly from coast to coast. Scientists and military experts were concerned that if the United States were attacked by the Soviet Union, its telephone communication system would be vulnerable. One missile could destroy the entire network of lines and wires that were needed for long-distance communication. A scientist from ARPA proposed a possible solution, suggesting that the United States design a network of computers that could talk to each other. If telephone systems were down, government leaders would be able to communicate with computers. At the same time, many scientists who needed to share their work and ideas with colleagues in other locations started thinking about ways to communicate through computers.

protocols

Sets of rules that governs the format of messages exchanged between computers.

With the help of computing experts and university scientists, ARPA devised a way for four computers running on different operating systems to "talk" to each other over a network. They called the network *ARPAnet*. The designers developed common sets of rules, or protocols, that the network followed so that the computers could communicate with each other without crashing the system. These early ARPAnet protocols evolved into many of the protocols that are used on the modern Internet.

Early computers, like the one pictured, could be big enough to fill an entire room. Yet they had far less processing power than today's much more compact machines, and were used primarily for calculation rather than communication.

In the 1970s and early 1980s scientists and researchers added more computers and networks to ARPAnet. This system of communication between computers and networks became the Internet. By the end of 1973 thirty institutions were connected to ARPAnet. Users included consulting firms, government sites, universities, and military research facilities.

As the Internet grew it connected millions of computers worldwide. The early Internet allowed people to communicate in small groups through networks that were closed to anyone who did not have permission to use them. Over time the Internet became an

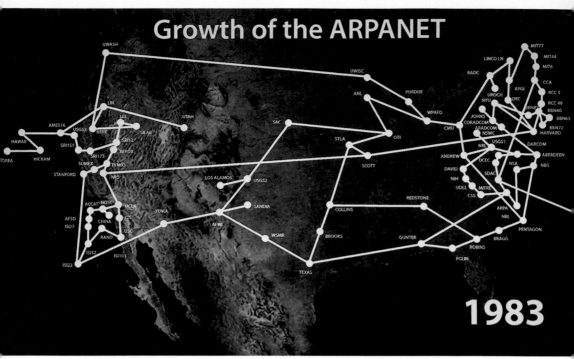

Growth of the ARPANET

1983

This map shows the locations of computers connected by ARPAnet in 1983. A precursor to today's Internet, ARPAnet was created to enable scientists and researchers to share their work with one another and to provide a way for US government entities to communicate via computer if the nation's telephone system ceased to function.

open network, and the number of people using it also increased. Users could connect more freely and publicly than ever before. As remarkable as the early Internet was, it was still limited. Computers were connected physically to the Internet through telephone lines and modems. Users were able to access the Internet only from desktop computer stations. In addition, getting information from the Internet was not always easy. Websites and web pages did not exist. Finding meaningful and useful information online was difficult for users without a technical background.

World Wide Web

The development of the Internet advanced significantly in 1991 with the introduction of the World Wide Web (WWW). Before the World Wide Web it was very difficult for someone on one computer system to look at anything other than text created by someone on another computer system. British computer scientist Tim Berners-Lee designed the World Wide Web. Berners-Lee wanted to make sure that information on the Internet could be easily accessed and used by anyone anywhere, no matter which computer and software they had available to them. What Berners-Lee designed is a system for creating, organizing, and linking documents and web pages on the Internet. He also designed a web page coding system, called HTML, and an addressing system that gave each web page a specific and unique location, or URL. The web made using the Internet easier for the average person. It simplified navigation on the Internet, giving users a tool and web addresses to navigate the massive network of computers. While the Internet connected computers around the world, the World Wide Web became the tool that allowed people to use those connections and communicate. With the web, Internet users could view information no matter what type of computer they were using. With the introduction of the web, the Internet became more accessible to the average person. Colleges and universities began to connect to the Internet. Businesses soon followed, along with everyday users in their homes.

In addition to the creation of the World Wide Web, the development of the web browser made the Internet easier to use. Web browser software communicates with Internet servers to get information. A web page's URL is the web address that tells the browser where to find the web page. The browser requests data from the server where the web page is stored. Then the browser translates the data and displays it in an easy-to-read format on a computer

web browser

Software that communicates with Internet servers to retrieve information.

screen. Browsers such as Internet Explorer and Netscape helped people of all ages, nationalities, and backgrounds use the Internet.

The development of search engines in the 1990s further increased the usability of the Internet. Before search engines, the Internet was a collection of websites that users had to navigate to find specific files. As the list of servers joining the Internet increased, it became increasingly hard for users to navigate the web servers and find files they wanted to access on the Internet.

Broadband Connections

At first, users connected to the Internet through a dial-up connection that ran through existing telephone lines. Dial-up connections were very slow, which made it difficult to download anything more than text. Using a dial-up connection, a single song of 3.5 megabytes (MB) often took anywhere from ten minutes to a few hours to download. If a user wanted to download a 700 MB movie, it took twenty-eight hours at full speed, or as much as several days. Dial-up connections were also inconvenient because users could not go online and use the telephone at the same time.

In the early 2000s the introduction of broadband connections transformed the Internet for many people. Broadband technology allows users to connect at faster speeds while not interfering with their telephone usage. Broadband allows the signal in the line to be split between telephone and Internet, so both can be used at the same time and at faster speeds. Broadband connections allowed users to download larger files, songs, and video content at faster speeds, opening a new world of online media. Broadband connections made sites like YouTube and Netflix possible.

Internet search engines helped to solve this problem. Search engines use automated software applications that travel through the web from site to site and gather information. The engines search sites based on important words and keep an index of the words they find and where they find them. When users type a single word or phrase into the search engine, it returns a list of websites where it has found those words and phrases.

Widespread Use

The introduction of the World Wide Web, web browsers, and search engines allowed the Internet to grow at a rapid pace in the 1990s and early 2000s. By 1998 more than 100 million users worldwide were using the Internet. By 2005 that number soared to over 1 billion users, according to the International Telecom Union (ITU), the United Nations specialized agency for information and communication technologies.

Around 2002 a new trend known as "Web 2.0" emerged. This refers to a change in how people used the Internet. Whereas once the Internet was mainly a source of information, by the early 2000s it became possible for users to create and upload their own content to the Internet. In this sense it became an interactive tool.

People created personal websites and blogs where they could post pictures, videos, music, and writing. They invited other users to view and comment on their content. Social networking sites such as Facebook and YouTube emerged, giving users even more avenues to share and upload their own content. These changes opened up a new world of possibilities for Internet communication and participation.

The Internet Today

Today the Internet has become more massive and complex than ever. It is a worldwide system of interconnected computer networks that link private, public, academic, business, and government networks. "The Internet is the decisive technology of the Information Age, and with the explosion of wireless communication in the early twenty-first century, we can say that humankind is now almost entirely connected,"[3] writes Manuel Castells, professor of communication technology and society at the University of Southern California.

URL

A web address.

The Internet's reach is expansive. Within a short period of time this technology has reached into homes, businesses, and lives. By the end of 2014 an estimated 3 billion people (or 40 percent of the world's population) were using the Internet. In developing countries the rate of Internet usage has increased at an astounding pace, with the number of users doubling between 2009 and 2014. In the United States the Internet reaches into almost every American home with 87 percent of American adults in 2014 using the Internet, according to the Pew Research Internet Project.

Today's users are no longer tied to a desktop computer to go online. Users access the Internet through a variety of electronic, wireless, and optical networking technologies. People surf the

Internet from their mobile phones while walking on the beach. They shop online on laptop or tablet computers anywhere in their homes. According to a 2014 report from the Pew Research Internet Project, 68 percent of American adults access the Internet on mobile devices such as smartphones or tablet computers.

Changing Life Worldwide

In the few decades since its introduction, the Internet and the World Wide Web have been embraced by millions of users worldwide. These technologies have had a significant impact on many aspects of daily life. They have changed how people get, share, and create news; how they communicate with family and friends; and the way they organize in communities. The Internet has also changed how many people perform their jobs, how they learn, and how they interact with their governments. Lee Rainie, director of the Pew Research Center's Internet & American Life Project, and Barry Wellman, director of NetLab at the University of Toronto, write:

> The volume of information is growing; the velocity of news (personal and formal) is increasing; the places where people can encounter others and information are proliferating; the ability of users to search for and find information is greater than ever; the tools allowing people to customize, filter, and assess information are more powerful; the capacity to create and share information is in more hands; and the potential for people to reach out to each other is unprecedented.[4]

The Internet has become embedded in daily life. This is what 53 percent of Internet users said in a 2014 Pew Research Internet Project report. This group said it would be very hard for them to give up the Internet. This increasing reliance on the Internet has developed over only a few years. In a 2006 Pew report only 38 percent of respondents said that it would be hard to give up the

Internet Use Has Exploded

Americans have steadily and rapidly adopted the Internet as an essential tool for communication, information-gathering, making purchases, organizing, entertainment, and more. This is borne out by Pew Research Center surveys conducted between 1995 and 2014. Survey results released in 2014 reveal that 87 percent of American adults now use the Internet. This is in contrast to only 14 percent who used the Internet in 1995.

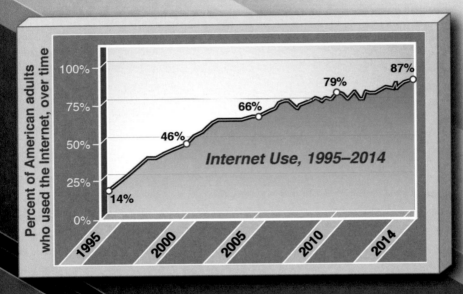

Internet. "In little more than a decade, the Internet has moved from being a plaything of computer scientists to becoming an important force in ordinary people's lives,"[5] write Rainie and Wellman.

Many Americans believe that the Internet has had a positive impact on their lives and society as a whole. According to the 2014 Pew report, 90 percent of Internet users said that the Internet has been a good thing for them personally. A slightly smaller number, 76 percent, said that they believed the Internet has been a good thing for society. At the same time, many people acknowledge that society is only beginning to understand the power of

Sending Packets

When a user tries to connect to a website to read an article, several things happen to make this possible. First, the computer sends an electronic request over an Internet connection to an Internet service provider (ISP). The ISP sends the request to a server further up the Internet chain. Eventually the request will hit a domain name server, where it will look for a match for the website name the user typed. If it finds a match, the server will send the user's request to the proper server's IP address. If it does not find a match, it will send the request back up the Internet chain to the next server.

Eventually, the request will reach the desired website's server. The server will send the requested file, broken into a series of packets. Packets are small parts of a file. Each packet has a header and footer that tell a computer what is in the packet and how it fits with other packets to create a file. Each packet travels along the network to the user's computer. Packets may take different paths to reach the same destination. This flexibility allows them to find a way around traffic jams on the Internet. Once all of the packets arrive, the user's computer arranges them according to the rules of Internet protocols. Once the requested article is complete, the user can read it. While this may sound like a lot of activity, the entire process actually happens almost instantaneously behind the computer screen.

the Internet, and they expect the future to hold more changes brought about by this transformative technology. Write authors Eric Schmidt and Jared Cohen,

> The Internet is among the few things humans have built that they don't truly understand. What began as a means of electronic information transmission—room-sized computer to room-sized computer—has transformed into an omnipresent and endlessly multifaceted outlet for human energy and expression. It is at once intangible and in a constant state of mutation, growing larger and more complex with each passing second. It is a source for tremendous good and potentially dreadful evil, and we're only just beginning to witness its impact on the world stage.[6]

Chapter Two

Opening the World and Sharing Online

Focus Questions

1. How has the Internet changed personal relationships and are these changes for the better? Explain your answer.
2. Why is the Internet described as a great leveler for businesses? What are the upsides and downsides of this?
3. How has the Internet changed news reporting, and are these changes for the better? Explain your answer.

"The Internet weaves the fabric of our lives. . . . We live in, on, and by the Internet."

—Manuel Castells, university professor and the Wallis Annenberg Chair in Communication Technology and Society at the University of Southern California (USC), Los Angeles.

Manuel Castells, foreword to *Society and the Internet: How Networks of Information and Communication Are Changing Our Lives*, edited by Mark Graham and William H. Dutton. New York: Oxford University Press, 2014, p. v.

The Internet has opened the world in many ways: connecting people, businesses, and countries faster and easier than at any other time in history. Through the Internet people enjoy free and easy access to all sorts of things from communication to commerce. There are more than 600 million websites worldwide and an estimated 3 billion people online. As a result, the Internet has changed the way people communicate, the way they work, and the way they go about their daily lives.

Making Communication Easier

Before the Internet, communicating with family, friends, and co-workers was slower and required more effort. People wrote letters to each other and sent them through the mail. No one expected an instantaneous response. In school, when students wanted to get messages to friends in the middle of class, they passed handwritten notes to each other. No one had cell phones in their purses or pockets. The fastest way to connect with someone was to use a landline or pay phone, but the caller could talk to only one person at a time. Coordinating Saturday night plans with a group of friends involved multiple phone calls and sometimes hours of planning time.

The introduction of the Internet has transformed the way people communicate, opening many new avenues. No longer limited to letters, telephone calls, or face-to-face meetings, people can send e-mail, text, or instant messages. They can post on social media, updating a Facebook status or tweeting news. Through VoIP users can make telephone calls through their Internet connections. Some services, such as Skype, enable video conferencing, allowing users to talk face-to-face while thousands of miles apart. Because many of these services are free or inexpensive, some people have dropped their landline telephone service entirely. According to a 2014 Gallup poll of American adults, texting, using a cell phone, and sending and reading e-mail messages are the most frequently used forms of communication. Between 37 and 39 percent of those surveyed said that they used each of these communication methods "a lot" each day. In comparison, less than 10 percent of respondents said that they used a home landline phone "a lot."

The advent of social media has also opened up numerous ways for people to communicate with friends and people who share common interests—no matter where they live. Across its many forms, social media's core purpose is sharing. On these sites people share photos, thoughts, videos, artwork, music, and

A Good Thing

Internet users overwhelmingly believe that both they and society have benefited from the ability to go online. The 2014 Pew Research Internet Project survey asked participants for their opinions on the pluses and minuses of the Internet. A whopping 90 percent responded that the Internet has been good for them as individuals, and a large number, 76 percent, said the Internet has been good for society.

Has the Internet been a good thing or a bad thing?

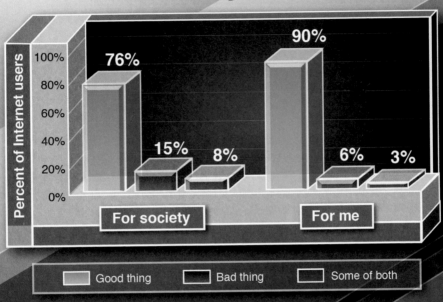

Source: Pew Research Center, "The Web at 25," February 2014. www.pewinternet.org.

more. Like e-mail, social media allows people to communicate more quickly, more easily, and more frequently.

With Internet technologies the speed and ease of communication has increased dramatically. Billions communicate with each other almost at any time, from almost any place. E-mails are delivered over the Internet almost instantaneously. Friends can instant message or text each other in a matter of seconds. Users can also send e-mails and texts to multiple recipients, reaching many people with just a few keystrokes. Attachments such as pictures, files, or videos can be delivered easily and quickly. And the ease of using Internet-connected mobile devices has allowed users to connect almost anywhere, at any time.

The Internet has also reduced the cost of communication. Before the Internet, a phone call to a person in another country incurred expensive long-distance fees, increasing with each minute of the call. Mailing letters overseas was also an expensive and slow process. In contrast, most online communications (especially e-mail and texting) cost very little beyond the price of an Internet connection. Users can even place overseas phone calls through the Internet using VoIP for no additional charge.

Building Relationships

New ways of communicating using the Internet have had an effect on human relationships. With so many ways to connect, the Internet and social media have helped people maintain and deepen existing relationships. According to Barry Wellman, director of NetLab at the University of Toronto, the many ways of communicating over the Internet have increased the overall frequency of communication. He states, "Online communication—email, instant messaging, chat rooms, etc.—does not replace more traditional offline forms of contact—face-to-face and telephone. Instead, it adds on to them, increasing the overall volume of contact."[7] In addition to meeting for lunch, friends post updates about their lives on Facebook, post pictures on Instagram, and message each other about social plans.

search engines

Software designed to look for information on the World Wide Web.

The Internet also makes it easier for people who are not geographically close to maintain relationships. With e-mails, texts, Skype, and other messaging apps, users can easily stay in touch with friends, family, and classmates who move out of town. Sarita Yardi, a computer science graduate student, says that the Internet has strengthened her relationships with family members and allows her to keep in touch with colleagues that she does not see on a regular basis. "I have 18 cousins, and most are married. Most have kids too and will often post pics. I've become closer— also in real world interactions—than I would otherwise be with all of them,"[8] she explains.

The Internet has also made it possible for people to form new relationships with people they have never met face-to-face. Before the Internet, geography limited an individual's social network. With the Internet's global reach, users can easily communicate with and get to know people who live halfway around the world. Today people are communicating and interacting with people from different countries, cultures, and backgrounds. From e-mail to social media, the Internet has transformed communication, making it global and instant.

Worldwide Information Sharing

Along with changing the way people communicate, the Internet has had a profound impact on how people find information about the world around them. A multitude of websites offer information on every subject imaginable. Search engines help users find the specific information that they want. From anywhere in the world people can go online to find phone numbers, recipes, store hours and locations, and how-to hints. Students use the Internet to research

African men in traditional dress make use of a laptop. Thanks to the Internet, people today can communicate with and befriend people around the globe whom they have never met in person.

topics for school reports, while scientists share information and reports about their latest work.

For many users the Internet has become a leading source of health and disease information. According to a 2013 survey by the Pew Research Center's Internet & American Life Project, 59 percent of American adults have gone online to research a medical condition. About half of the searches were performed on behalf of another person. Physicians Jerome Groopman and Pamela Hartzband say that the Internet gives people more control over health decisions. In the process, the Internet is changing the roles of the doctor and patient. Say Groopman and Hartzband:

> Information traditionally flowed from doctor to patient; the physician described the genesis and course of a disease and the options available for treating it. Often, pamphlets were provided to reinforce the doctor's explanation and advice. The patient might then receive additional input from family and friends, usually in the form of anecdotes about people who faced similar clinical situations.

> The Internet has upended that scenario. The Web offers virtually unlimited amounts of information. Everyone can now visit many of the sites that inform and educate doctors. Popular search engines such as Google and Yahoo provide portals to primary data published in scholarly journals as well as critical analyses of these studies, slide presentations from grand rounds, videos of surgical procedures, and guidelines from professional societies.[9]

In some cases an Internet health search can save a life. In 2010 San Diego Padres pitcher Tim Stauffer was suffering from severe abdominal pain. Stauffer used his iPhone to research his symptoms on a health website. Based on the information he found, Stauffer correctly suspected he had appendicitis. He went to the hospital and underwent surgery to remove his appendix.

Breaking News

Before the Internet, people read newspapers and magazines, listened to radio programs, or watched television to stay informed

Tweeting in a Disaster

When Hurricane Sandy devastated the northeastern United States in 2012, Twitter became an information lifeline. Many people affected by the storm had lost power but were still able to access the Internet via smartphones and other mobile devices. According to Twitter, people sent more than 20 million tweets about the storm during its first days, from October 27 through November 1. A full 34 percent of the tweets involved news and information about the storm from news organizations, government sources, and eyewitnesses, according to a study by the Pew Research Center's Project for Excellence in Journalism. The second largest share of tweets over the first three days of the storm involved people sharing photos and videos of the storm and its devastation.

about current events. With the Internet there has been a dramatic shift in how people learn about current events. Now websites report breaking news from around the globe with blinding speed. Blogs offer different perspectives, opinions, and analysis on countless topics and issues. Community Listservs (automatic electronic mailing lists) feature news and information of local interest.

With all of these choices more people are turning to the Internet for news. According to a 2013 study by the Pew Research Center, 50 percent of the American public say that the Internet has become their main source for national and international news, coming in second behind television (69 percent), but ahead of newspapers (28 percent) and radio (23 percent). For younger Americans, however, the Internet has surpassed even television as the most popular source of news. Of those aged eighteen to twenty-nine, 71 percent reported that the Internet was their main news source.

Listservs

Automatic electronic mailing lists.

Many people are getting news from Internet-connected mobile devices. Users can read news feeds from their phones, receive alerts about breaking news, and access websites anywhere they go. According to a survey by the Pew Research Center's Project for

Excellence in Journalism (PEJ) in collaboration with the Economist Group, 64 percent of computer tablet owners and 62 percent of smartphone owners report that they read news on their devices at least weekly. Furthermore, these users are doing more than scanning headlines on their mobile devices. Many are reading longer news stories and in-depth articles on a regular basis. For some people the ability to access news from the palm of their hands on a mobile device has increased the overall amount of news they read. More than four in ten mobile news consumers report that they are getting more news than before, while nearly one-third report that they have added additional news sources.

news feeds

Constantly updated lists of content.

Although the Internet delivers news faster and farther than ever before, the quality and accuracy of online news sources varies widely. Anyone can upload content to the Internet. While most professional news organizations check facts and vet sources before reporting a news story, many websites feature articles and information that have not been checked for accuracy. In addition, the line between fact and opinion is often blurred online, with many opinionated articles being represented as factual and unbiased.

Social Media and News

While many people go to official news websites, such as the *New York Times* Online, social media is quickly becoming a major source of news online. Nearly 50 percent of Internet users reported in 2014 that they regularly or occasionally heard about a breaking news story on social media. Social media sites have been the first to report several high-interest news stories in recent years, including the engagement of Britain's Prince William, the death of legendary singer Whitney Houston, and the 2013 Boston Marathon bombing.

Social media giant Facebook is the largest social networking site among American adults, and its reach for spreading news is wide. Facebook executives embrace the site's role as a provider of news and have taken steps to shift the content of users' news feeds to include hard news along with status updates from friends.

Britain's Prince William and his wife, Kate Middleton, Duchess of Cambridge, wave to the public after their 2011 wedding. The couple's engagement was first reported on social media rather than through traditional news sources.

In 2014 the company announced the creation of Newswire, an official Facebook page that users can follow, which aggregates the best original content posted on the site. The company envisions Newswire as a tool for journalists looking for primary sources about news events, but it can also be followed by the average user. Stories posted to Newswire will appear in a user's news feed. "It's all about thinking of Facebook as a primary source of news content, formatted so journalists can easily scan content and pick out what's newsworthy," says Andy Mitchell, director of news and global media partnerships at Facebook. "But it's not just for news breaking. I would also look at it as complementary content to big stories of the day."[10]

Along with reading news, social media users are sharing and adding to it. Half of social media users say they have shared news stories, images, or videos. Slightly less than half (46 percent) say they have discussed a news story on a social media site. A small

Digital Activism

The Internet has provided a new tool for political protest. Digital activism is the practice of using digital technology for political and social change. Sometimes people use the Internet to organize groups and mobilize offline activities, protests, and events. Other times, protests take place mainly online, often through social media sites.

The Internet enables activists to carry out activities more quickly, on a larger scale, and at a lower cost. For example, an e-petition collects signatures as does a paper petition but can be distributed quickly and cheaply, and signed by anyone at any time. After the 2012 killing of Trayvon Martin, an African American teen in Florida, a Change.org e-petition calling for justice and the prosecution of his killer collected more than 2 million signatures in only two weeks. The state of Florida arrested and brought Martin's shooter to trial, although he was eventually acquitted by a jury.

The Internet also gives ordinary people the ability to lead and participate in activism without formal organizations. Beginning in 2011 the Occupy movement protested social and economic inequality around the world. Individuals in different communities staged multiple protests, using web technologies and social media to coordinate the events.

number are adding to the news, uploading pictures or videos of news events. This practice has played a role in the reporting of breaking news events. During an emergency or natural disaster, social media sites have become an information hotline. News organizations post content, government officials release critical information, and everyday people share eyewitness accounts and information via Facebook, Twitter, and other social media sites.

Global Businesses

The ability to communicate and reach people around the world has also transformed business and significantly expanded the opportunities for modern companies. Before the Internet, a company opened a physical store and advertised to local residents via newspapers, television and radio, or direct mail. Businesses were limited geographically, with customers usually being located close to physical stores. A clothing store sold its goods to customers who visited the store during specific store hours. Its survival depended on whether or not local people bought the items being sold in the store.

With the Internet, businesses of all types and sizes have the ability to attract customers globally. With a website presence, a business can sell its goods and services to customers no matter where they are, increasing its customer base. The Internet has changed how products are designed, produced, and distributed. Even the smallest companies can purchase supplies or hire employees from different regions and even countries. According to James Manyika and Charles Roxburgh:

> The Internet's biggest impact on SMEs [small and medium enterprises] has been as a great leveler, making it possible for a small firm to be a global company from day one, with the reach and capabilities that once only large companies could possess. They can reach customers, find suppliers, and tap talent on the other side of the world and can also use the Internet to provide significant marketing and brand muscle. As a result, small firms can compete like big ones.[11]

For many companies the Internet has stimulated revenue and growth. A McKinsey Global Institute survey of forty-eight hundred companies from twelve countries found that small and medium companies that used web technologies grew more than twice as fast as those with a minimal web presence. In addition, web-utilizing companies brought in more than twice as much revenue from exports as a percentage of total sales than those who rarely used the Internet.

AFG Media is a UK company that created the Morphsuit, an all-in-one spandex suit that covers the body from head to toe. Morphsuits have become popular costumes at parties and other events. In the company's first year in 2009 it earned revenues of £1.2 million (British pounds). By 2012 revenues had soared to £11 million, and the company expanded internationally. The company's founders credit the Internet for their success. "Without Facebook, we simply would not exist in the way we do today," says Gregor Lawson, one of the company's founding directors. With little money for advertising and marketing, AFG built a community of customers through its Facebook page. It posted photos of people wearing Morphsuits and organized competitions. The founders reasoned that the more people participated on their Facebook page, the more likely they would make a purchase later. "People underestimate the commercial power of Facebook," says Lawson. "For every one person who does something on our page, another nine will 'like' it and another 90 will see what's been done. People think social media is flitty. I disagree—if you're clear about your objectives and your customers, you can deliver real commercial advantages on Facebook."[12]

E-Commerce

The Internet has even sparked a new business model—electronic commerce, or e-commerce. E-commerce is the buying and selling of products and services by businesses and consumers through the Internet. It includes many types of businesses, such as consumer retail websites, music sites, and services. Some companies operate exclusively online without a physical store. Others have added e-commerce and the ability to sell online to their existing stores, allowing them to reach more customers. As more people use smartphones and other mobile devices to go online, e-commerce continues to expand. According to a 2014 report from Forrester Research, US e-retail sales are expected to grow from $263 billion in 2013 to $414 billion in 2018, with e-retail's share of total sales increasing from 8 percent to 11 percent over that period.

> **e-commerce**
>
> Buying and selling of products and services through the Internet.

At the same time, the Internet's effect on business has not been positive for all companies. As more people turn to shopping online, many brick-and-mortar stores have seen their revenues drop, and some have gone out of business. For example, the emergence of Amazon as an online bookstore has triggered the closure of many traditional bookstores across the country. These companies were unable to adapt to new Internet-driven business models.

Transforming Life

In many ways the Internet has changed how people learn about the world and interact with each other. These changes have also affected society's expectations. Today most people expect to be able to find information on almost any subject quickly and easily. People also expect to be reachable at more times and places than in the past and assume that others will also be available.

The Internet has also made the world a smaller place, bringing people from all countries and backgrounds together online. "To be sure, neighbors and neighborhoods still exist, but they occupy a smaller portion of people's lives. It is hard to borrow a cup of sugar from a Facebook friend 1,000 miles away but it has become easier to socialize, get advice, and exchange emotional support at any distance,"[13] say Lee Rainie and Barry Wellman. With all of these changes, the Internet has had a significant impact on society.

Chapter Three

Who Controls Information Online?

Focus Questions

1. How has the Internet compromised personal privacy?
2. How important is personal privacy to you? Does Internet use justify the loss of personal privacy? Explain your thinking.
3. What effect does website tracking have on individual behavior online, and why does this matter?

"We can now be tracked in time and space with a degree of precision that would make tyrants of days past envious."

—Ronald J. Deibert, professor of political science and director of the Canada Centre for Global Security Studies and the Citizen Lab at the Munk School of Global Affairs, University of Toronto.

Ronald J. Deibert, *Black Code: Surveillance, Privacy and the Dark Side of the Internet*. Toronto, ON: McClelland & Stewart, 2013, p. 5.

Every time users go online, information about their identities, likes and dislikes, locations, shopping habits, and more becomes part of their digital footprints. Once those details are online, users can quickly lose control over how their information is used.

Decreasing Personal Privacy

Internet users willingly hand over volumes of personal information when they are online. To sign up for frequent shopper programs or e-mail alerts, users enter information into website forms. On social media sites they update statuses, upload pictures, and give details about their likes, dislikes, and daily habits. The volume of personal information making its way online through social media sites is astounding. In a typical day users upload an average of 350 million pictures on Facebook alone. On Instagram users post 35 million selfies per day—more than four hundred per second. And Twitter users send more than 400 million tweets per day. "The unspoken issue is that we're creating a digital trail of all we say and do. For the first time in history, we're documenting everything without regard to where or how these records are kept and backed up. Our data has an eternal life, with each of us serving as our own personal historians, many times without even knowing it,"[14] says Nat Maple, senior vice president and general manager at Acronis, a company that provides global data protection solutions.

The decrease in privacy is greater than the information shared in website forms or social media sites. Almost every time a user logs on to a website, someone is looking over his or her shoulder. Behind the scenes, businesses, Internet service providers, search engines, and other companies track what users do online. These entities gather information such as a user's location, address, name, e-mail, and phone number. They track what sites a user visits, what keywords he or she uses for online searches, and what his or her specific shopping habits are.

By tracking a user's online movements, the companies can build a profile of the user, including detailed information such as religious beliefs, political affiliations, finances, race, ethnic background, and health concerns. The websites and news articles a person reads can give clues about his or her political views. Other activities can reveal which social causes a person supports, what type of music he or she likes, and even what genre of books he or she reads. This information can be used by companies to target marketing toward customers. It can also be sold to data brokers, who have created an entire industry, known as Big Data, that is devoted to collecting personal details. Big Data takes these details and matches them to real-life activities

Big Data

An industry that collects and analyzes large amounts of data.

A smartphone displays the social networking service Instagram. Instagram users post a total of 35 million pictures of themselves, or "selfies," every day. Security experts worry that most such postings are made without regard for the privacy issues they could create.

to predict how people will vote in the next election, what type of car they might purchase, or whether they are a good insurance risk.

Many people acknowledge the trade-off between personal privacy and the Internet. Many users know that their online activities are being tracked to some degree, but they view it as an acceptable compromise for being able to fully use and customize the web, social media, and other technologies. "It's a trade-off," says Bill Scully, a forty-seven-year-old Internet user from Boston. "When you sign up for Google Inc.'s Gmail, for example, you get free email in exchange for letting the company target ads to you. The same with Facebook. When you sign up for Facebook, you are basically signing up for a big marketing survey."[15]

Data Permanence

Before the Internet, pictures from a party, letters to a boyfriend or girlfriend, or medical test results existed only on paper. A limited number of people had access to these things, which could be locked away or destroyed if a person did not want others to see them. With the Internet it is much more difficult, if not impossible, to delete or lock away information once it is online. A user can delete a Facebook post or Instagram photo, but someone may

> **data permanence**
>
> The expected lifetime of data in the digital world.

have already taken a screenshot of it and saved it and passed it on. Website backups can also retain deleted data. In this way, all of a user's online activity and associations as well as his or her personal information, financial and medical data, status updates, photos, videos, and tweets become part of a permanent vault of online information. "This will be the first generation of humans to have an indelible record,"[16] write Eric Schmidt and Jared Cohen.

Once data becomes permanent online there is a real risk that people will lose control of how and where their data is used. With increasing frequency online data is being shared, leaked, or stolen. Even knowing these risks, many people continue to post personal information online. Partly this is because thoughts about privacy have changed. In particular, studies show that teens and young adults do not place as high a value on personal privacy as earlier generations. This worries some experts, who say that the public should be more concerned with maintaining control over personal information. "The bottom line is: if our digital records live in perpetuity, we need to take more ownership and control over where and how we choose to keep them,"[17] says Maple.

Cloud Data Concerns

As more people take photos, make videos, and create content with mobile devices, the need for more data storage has exploded. In addition, as more users own multiple devices—from smartphones to tablets—they want to be able share their content and access it from any device. To solve these problems many users and Internet services store data in the cloud. Cloud storage is a service that maintains, manages, and stores data remotely on third-party servers, making it available to users over the Internet. Instead of saving photos and documents on a personal computer's hard drive or on a thumb drive, people who use cloud storage save data on third-party servers located anywhere around the world. Web-based e-mail services, files stored in Google Drive, and pictures uploaded to Snapfish are all stored in the cloud.

cloud storage

A service that maintains, manages, and stores data remotely on third-party servers.

Cloud storage is taking the online world by storm. By 2016, 36 percent of consumer digital content will be stored in the cloud compared to only 7 percent of consumer content in 2011, according to Gartner, Inc., an information technology research and advisory company. "Historically, consumers have generally stored content on their PCs, but as we enter the post-PC era, consumers are using multiple connected devices, the majority of which are equipped with cameras. This is leading to a massive increase in new user-generated content that requires storage,"[18] says Shalini Verma, a principal research analyst at Gartner. Verma says that the arrival of the cloud as a way to store this user-generated content will cause more data to become separated from users' devices and control.

With more information in the cloud, concerns over security and privacy of data are increasing. To begin with, data stored in the cloud is not legally protected in the same way as data on a personal computer's hard drive. In the United States the Fourth Amendment to the Constitution protects citizens from "unreasonable searches and seizures." In practice this means that law enforcement and the government must have a warrant and provide probable cause that a crime has been committed before they can

A fan uses a smartphone to take pictures at a baseball game. The creation of pictures and videos that are shared across devices has exploded in recent years, producing a need for data storage solutions beyond the traditional method of saving files on a PC's hard drive.

access personal data and files. This Fourth Amendment protection, however, makes an exception in cases where data is stored with a third party. A person cannot claim something is private if it is stored with a third party. "A huge concern about using the cloud is that your data does not have the same Fourth Amendment protections that it would have if it were stored in a desk drawer or even your desktop computer,"[19] says John M. Simpson, director of the Privacy Project at Consumer Watchdog.

Law enforcement agencies have increasingly applied this third-party exemption to data in the cloud. According to Google's *Transparency Report*, the company has experienced an increase in requests from governments and courts for cloud-based data,

Tracking Cookies

One of the most common ways that companies and websites track users' online movements is through the use of web browser cookies. A cookie is a small text file that web servers store on a user's hard drive. Cookies allow websites to track a user's movements within a site and gather information the user voluntarily gives on the site. With cookies, websites can remember a user's preferences and create a profile for future marketing. Web experts warn that cookies are multiplying across the web, with advertising networks, marketers, and other data brokers relying on cookies to learn more about potential consumers. "Five to ten years ago, if you opened NYT.com in your browser, you'd get a cookie from the New York Times, maybe a couple, and that would basically be it," says staff technologist Dan Auerbach of the Electronic Frontier Foundation, a nonprofit organization focused on protecting civil liberties in the digital world. "Today you get probably on the order of 50 cookies from all sorts of third parties: ad servers, data brokers, trackers. They can build up this big profile about your browsing history." The worst part, he says, is that "it's totally invisible to users. They have no idea what's happening." Marketers claim that user privacy fears are overblown because they keep user data private and only view it in aggregate. Still, the sheer volume of information that cookies collect about any single user can jeopardize a user's privacy and anonymity.

Quoted in Melissa Riofrio, "The 5 Biggest Online Privacy Threats of 2013," *PC World*, April 8, 2013. www.pcworld.com.

from 12,539 requests during the last six months of 2009 to 31,698 requests in the first six months of 2014. "The only true protection is to understand that anything you put up there can be accessed by somebody else," says Simpson. "If you don't want that to happen, don't put it in the cloud."[20]

In 2014 cloud security made headlines when dozens of celebrities fell victim to a hacker who invaded their iCloud accounts and leaked embarrassing photos. The hacker took advantage of a security flaw in Apple's iCloud online backup service. "Certain celebrity accounts were compromised by a very targeted attack on user names, passwords and security questions, a practice that has become all too common on the Internet,"[21] Apple says. When actress Mary E. Winstead discovered that her iCloud backup account was among those hacked, she tweeted, "Knowing those photos were deleted long ago, I can only imagine the creepy effort that went into this. Feeling for everyone who got hacked."[22]

Location, Location, Location

Internet-connected devices and apps are revealing more than just personal information; they can also reveal a user's physical location. Cell phones transmit location data, showing where and when a person travels from place to place. Social networking sites and various apps can also reveal a user's location. Users who "check in" through a social media site when they arrive at a restaurant or store, for example, are essentially announcing where their location is to anyone who has access to their page. With all of these devices and apps, users can be tracked from the minute they leave their homes in the morning to when they return late at night. "When you leave your house and go to a friend's house, run errands, go to work, visit a lover—whatever it is you do—if your geolocation is tracked and recorded, that's a lot of information about you,"[23] says senior policy analyst Jay Stanley of the American Civil Liberties Union's Speech, Privacy and Technology Program.

How this data is being used can vary. In some cases local businesses use location data to track nearby potential customers and send them up-to-the minute promotions. For example, a restaurant might send an e-mail or text about that evening's dinner specials. Other times law enforcement, employers, or former spouses use location data to track users. Lillie Coney, the associate director of the Electronic Privacy Information Center, warns that users may not like what employers are tracking about them. She says that an employer-owned device "lets your employer track you, on and off the job. What kind of consequences and profile data are based on your geolocation, based on the course of your time in or out of work, where you are, how late you are?"[24] Government agencies can also access a user's location data without his or her knowledge. According to Electronic Frontier Foundation (EFF) staff attorney Jennifer Lynch, "It's pretty easy for the government to get access to the location data, and very hard for users to prevent that data from being gathered."[25] While it is unclear exactly how often the government is accessing location data without users' knowledge, the American Civil Liberties Union (ACLU) estimates that there are thousands, and possibly tens of thousands, of cases in which it is occurring.

Dangerous Consequences

Once a user's personal details are online it is not possible to control how that information is used. In many cases businesses and Big Data harvest online information for targeted advertising. Other times the loss of personal information can be dangerous. Predators, cybercriminals, bullies, and others can take advantage of unwary Internet users. Thieves who invent scams, hustles, and cons to trick victims out of money are nothing new. With the Internet's power and reach, however, these criminals can access billions of potential victims in a few seconds. Anyone who uses the Internet can become a victim regardless of age, gender, or location.

Identity thieves use victims' personal information to steal money through identity theft. Identity theft is the misuse of credit card, bank account, or other personal information to commit fraud. Using names, addresses, Social Security numbers, financial and bank account numbers, passwords, and other details, thieves pretend to be their victims. Identity thieves can gain access to personal information in several ways. Some hack into business or individual computer databases to steal information. Others send phishing e-mails or pop-up messages that trick consumers into handing over personal or financial information. Some savvy thieves trick users into providing personal information through fake websites that look identical to the real sites. Others download malicious programs called spyware from the Internet onto a user's personal computer; spyware collects personal information and sends it to the thieves.

identity theft

Misuse of another person's personal information to commit fraud.

Monica Hamilton, a marketing director at cybersecurity firm McAfee, Inc., warns that identity theft has become big business for online thieves. She says that the number of malicious programs written to steal a user's information has grown from about 1 million in 2007 to an estimated 130 million in 2013. When thieves hack into businesses to steal credit card numbers and other personal information, the losses suffered by the targeted companies can be significant. Businesses have to pay for legal settlements, consultant fees to remove malware from company computers and servers, and personnel hours for those working to resolve problems and notify customers.

In 2013 Kelly Droste, a Maricopa, Arizona, resident, learned that an identity thief had stolen her personal information and filed a tax return in her name to steal her tax refund. She reported the fraud but was told it would take at least six months to resolve the issue. During that time, her $2,700 refund was also delayed. Droste

The Internet has enabled criminals to target victims in a variety of ways, including making unauthorized purchases using stolen credit card numbers and creating fraudulent credit card accounts in a victim's name.

learned that identity thieves had also attempted to open credit card accounts in her name. She has spent dozens of hours trying to block the fraudulent applications and has filed a police report.

Victims like Droste can suffer in many ways. In addition to dealing with the inconvenience of having to replace all existing credit and debit cards, victims can spend years trying to clear their credit record and remove bad debt run up by identify thieves under their names. Some are unable to borrow money or get a mortgage because of the damage to their credit history. Others have have had to file bankruptcy and have lost their homes.

Cyberbullies

With more sharing and social interaction taking place online, the Internet has created a new place for bullying. Cyberbullying occurs when a bully uses the Internet, cell phones, computers, and other digital technologies to harass and threaten others. Cyberbullying can occur on social media sites, in text messages and chat rooms, and on websites. It can take many forms, from threatening text messages to embarrassing pictures posted on social media or websites. Unlike traditional bullying, which is limited to face-to-face contact with a known bully, cyberbullying can be anonymous, and the attacks can happen online at any time or place.

With more people, especially teens, online cyberbullying has become a growing problem. According to the Cyberbullying Research Center, about 25 percent of high school and middle school students in the United States report that they have been victims of cyberbullying, with girls being more likely than boys to experience cyberbullying. Cyberbullying can have serious consequences. Victims report low self-esteem, anger, frustration, and other emotional and psychological problems. In some extreme cases victims have committed suicide.

Experts say that awareness of cyberbullying is the key to prevention. Many schools have implemented antibullying programs that include discussions of cyberbullying and appropriate online behavior. They hope that educating kids and parents about cyberbullying will help put a stop to it.

Real-World Crime

In some cases losing control of information online can make users vulnerable to the real-world threats of stalkers, predators, and burglars. In particular, the sharing of personal information on social media can put users at risk. Police investigator Joe Baeza of Laredo, Texas, says although it is fun to stay in touch with friends in the virtual world, it can cause problems in the real world. "The accessibility is there. There's all kinds of free information for the person who knows how to find it on the internet. So, be very, very careful. Be extremely conscious of the fact that the more information you make available to people on social media, the more the risk you run to have the wrong person get that information."[26]

In 2014 Cliff Ford of Toronto, Canada, helped police track and arrest a predator who had been stalking his twelve-year-old daughter over the Internet. Nicholas Bowers, a thirty-year-old man from Ohio, had befriended Ford's daughter in an online chat room and had begun sending her sexually suggestive e-mails and chat messages. After Ford discovered one of the e-mails, he pretended to be his daughter online, chatting with Bowers and eventually getting his full name, address, place of work, and the type of car he drove. "I basically took over my daughter's profile and conversed with this guy in the chat room—as my daughter—to try and get as much information as I could,"[27] he says. Ford gave the information he had gathered to local police in the United States. With the help of Toronto police they investigated, raided, and arrested Bowers on child exploitation charges. "Attentive parents and swift law enforcement action has ensured that Mr. Bowers will not be trolling for minors on the Internet," says FBI special agent Stephen D. Anthony. "This international collaborative law enforcement effort demonstrates that preying on our most precious commodity, our children, will not be tolerated."[28]

Risk vs. Reward

While the Internet has brought many benefits to society, it has also introduced risks that users need to be aware of and understand. Some people, including security expert Bruce Schneier, are alarmed over the negative impact of the Internet on society, particularly its effect on privacy. Schneier warns,

> Welcome to a world where Google knows . . . more about your interests than your spouse does. Welcome to a world where your cellphone company knows exactly where you are all the time. Welcome to the end of private conversations, because increasingly your conversations are conducted by email, text, or social networking sites. And welcome to a world where all of this, and everything else that you do or is done on a computer, is saved, correlated, studied, passed around from company to company without your knowledge or consent; and where the government accesses it at will without a warrant. Welcome to an Internet without privacy, and we've ended up here with hardly a fight.[29]

Because the Internet is still a young and evolving technology, some people believe that growing pains are to be expected. Trevor Hughes, CEO of the International Association of Privacy Professionals, compares the early days of the Internet to the early days of the Industrial Revolution and says that each has its share of issues and concerns. "But the industrial revolution ultimately resulted in things like the five-day work week and child labor laws," he says. "One of the first issues we have to grapple with in the information economy is privacy, but I expect there will be dozens more."[30] Hughes believes that ultimately the benefits of the Internet will outweigh its risks.

Chapter Four

Regulating the Internet

Focus Questions

1. Do you think that Internet censorship is ever justified? Why or why not?
2. What effect, if any, would more restrictive regulations have on the Internet—both nationally and globally?
3. The leaders of some countries view the Internet as a threat; others view it as a benefit. How do these views affect decisions about Internet regulation?

"The growing restrictions at the national level are also changing the nature of the global internet, transforming it from a worldwide network into a fragmented mosaic, with both the rules and the accessible content varying from one country to another."

—Sanja Kelly, project director at Freedom House, an independent watchdog organization dedicated to expanding freedom around the world.

Sanja Kelly et al., "Freedom on the Net 2014," Freedom House, 2014. www.freedomhouse.org.

No single entity, government, or country owns the Internet. In some ways, the Internet is "owned" by the billions of people around the world who use it every day. Because control is spread across many parties, regulation of the Internet often depends on where a user lives. With so many users and no single owner, the question of how to regulate it and who is responsible has become increasingly complex and difficult to answer.

Internet Governance

In the early years of the Internet, the idea of Internet governance mainly meant coordinating global users and managing domain names and IP addresses. Internet users come from different countries and speak different languages. In order for the world's computer networks to communicate over the Internet, there has to be a standard set of rules and vocabulary. Without these rules, the global computer networks would not be able to communicate with each other. Many entities work together to keep the Internet operating. Several organizations oversee the Internet's infrastructure and protocols, including the Internet Society, the Internet Engineering Task Force (IETF), the Internet Architecture Board (IAB), and the Internet Corporation for Assigned Names and Numbers (ICANN).

domain name

Used to identify one or more IP addresses, such as yahoo.com.

As Internet use has expanded, however, the idea of Internet governance has also expanded. Today many people have a part in defining and carrying out Internet governance. People, organizations, companies, and governments work together to develop and apply shared principles, norms, rules, procedures, and programs that shape the use of the Internet. Tens of thousands of entities, including network and server operators, domain name registrars, IP address and standards organizations, service providers, individual users, industry organizations, and governments all contribute to governance and developing policies for Internet use.

Government and the Internet

Although no country can regulate the entire Internet, governments can pass Internet-related policies for use within a country's borders. In the Internet's early years, few countries had laws specifically to regulate information and communication technologies (ICTs). As people began to communicate online, especial-

An Internet café in China is shown packed with users. China is one of several countries whose governments view the Internet as a threat and attempt to restrict the kinds of online content that are available to their citizens.

ly through social media, an increasing number of governments passed new laws or amended existing ones to regulate speech and activity online.

When deciding how to regulate the Internet, different countries view the benefits and risks differently. The governments of China and Iran, for instance, view the Internet as a threat and believe it should be strongly controlled. Governments with this point of view may choose to censor political and social content online, restricting what is available to their citizens. According to a 2013 report by the independent watchdog group Freedom House, since 2012 twenty-four countries have passed laws or regulations that restrict free speech online, that violate user privacy, or that punish individuals who post certain types of content.

Governments in other countries, including the United States and Canada, support an open Internet. An open Internet is one that can be accessed by anyone who wishes to use it and that treats all traffic that flows across it in a similar way, without restricting content.

Yet even in open countries lawmakers have proposed legislation to regulate some aspects of Internet use.

Restrictive Regulation

According to the Freedom House report, Internet freedom is declining in countries around the world. In a 2013 report that followed sixty countries, analysts found that many governments use tactics such as broad surveillance of online activity, legislation controlling and restricting web content, and arrests of social media users to limit Internet freedom. For the second consecutive year, the report found that China, Cuba, and Iran were the most repressive countries for Internet freedom. The report stated that twenty-nine of the sixty countries evaluated blocked certain types of political and social content. China, Iran, and Saudi Arabia are among the countries cited for blocking large amounts of content. Even democratic countries such as South Korea and India blocked some websites with political content. "While blocking and filtering remain the preferred methods of censorship in many countries, governments are increasingly looking at who is saying what online, and finding ways to punish them," says Sanja Kelly, project director for *Freedom on the Net* at Freedom House. "In some countries, a user can get arrested for simply posting on Facebook or for "liking" a friend's comment that is critical of the authorities,"[31] she adds.

> **regulation**
>
> A law or rule designed to control or govern conduct.

According to the report, many governments passed laws prohibiting certain types of political, religious, or social speech online. In 2013 twenty-eight countries arrested users for online content that violated these restrictions. The arrests included political dissidents and people who posted comments on social media that criticized the country's authorities or major religion. As Kelly notes,

Of particular concern are the proliferation of laws, regulations, and directives to restrict online speech; a dramatic increase in arrests of individuals for something they posted online; legal cases and intimidation against social-media users; and a rise in surveillance. In authoritarian states, these tools are often used to censor and punish users who engage in online speech that is deemed critical of the government, royalty, or the dominant religion. In some countries, even blogging about environmental pollution, posting a video of a cynical rap song, or tweeting about the town mayor's poor parking could draw the police to a user's door.[32]

In 2012 Bahrain police arrested at least ten Twitter users and charged them with "insulting the king on Twitter." Several of those arrested received prison sentences from one to four months.

Privacy Legislation

Little federal legislation currently regulates online privacy and the growing online consumer data industry. In January 2015 President Barack Obama proposed several privacy laws that would give Americans more control over their personal information. One proposed act forbids companies from using student data—which is collected when companies sell software and services to primary and secondary schools—for marketing purposes. Another proposal would require retailers, banks, and other companies to notify customers of data breaches within thirty days of learning of the breach.

Until the federal government acts, several states have taken on the issue of online privacy regulation, passing their own laws to regulate privacy on the Internet. In Texas the state legislature passed a law in 2013 that requires state law enforcement to obtain a search warrant before accessing e-mails and other forms of electronic communications content from service providers. Also in 2013, Maine's state legislature passed a law that requires police to get a search warrant before tracking a person through a cell phone or other electronic device. Other states have banned employers from asking for logins and passwords to the personal social media, e-mail, and other online accounts of their current and prospective employees.

Some countries have blocked access to social media entirely. According to the 2013 Freedom House report, nineteen countries completely blocked at least one blogging, microblogging, video-sharing, social networking, or live streaming platform. Many specifically targeted and blocked YouTube, Twitter, and Facebook either temporarily or permanently. Some governments have also blocked access to individual pages or profiles on social media. VoIP and free services such as Skype and WhatsApp are also frequently blocked because government authorities find it difficult to intercept and monitor these communication apps.

A few governments have even shut down or slowed Internet or mobile phone service in a town, region, or entire country. In 2011 Egyptian officials shut down the Internet for five days when protesters called for the removal of longtime president Hosni

Protesters in Egypt call for the resignation of president Hosni Mubarak during an uprising in 2011. In response to such protests, Mubarak's government shut down the Internet in the country for five days.

Mubarak. In Venezuela the government-controlled main ISP shut down service during the country's 2013 presidential election, leaving citizens disconnected from online news and information and unable to track election results. This shutdown also prevented the international community from learning about the election results in real time. In other cases some countries use throttling, or purposely slowing down Internet connection speeds, to prevent users from uploading videos or viewing websites.

Regulation in the United States

In the United States access to the Internet remains relatively free compared with more restrictive countries. Access to the Internet is generally unregulated, and Americans face few restrictions on their ability to publish content online. The US court system has consistently ruled that free speech protections under the US Constitution also include speech on the Internet.

In the United States several agencies are responsible for regulating different aspects of the technology and its use. The Federal Communications Commission (FCC), the agency that is responsible for regulating radio and television broadcasts, interstate communications, and international communications that begin or end in the United States, claims jurisdiction over some Internet communication issues. Other government agencies, such as the National Telecommunications and Information Administration (NTIA), are involved with telecommunications and technology policies and regulations that involve the Internet. In addition, Congress creates laws that govern the Internet.

intellectual property

A creation of the mind, such as music, art, and inventions.

Although the US government does not restrict access to political or social content online, some laws regulating Internet use have been proposed, and several have been passed. Most of these laws exist to regulate real-world activities and now extend to cover activities on the Internet. For example, Congress has passed legislation to address issues such as protecting minors online, protecting intellectual property, free speech rights, and online harassment and threats.

Protecting Minors Online

Protecting children from indecent or harmful content while online has been the focus of several pieces of legislation in the United States. In 1996 the United States passed the Communications Decency Act (CDA), which attempted to regulate indecency and obscenity online. In 1998 Congress passed the Child Online Protection Act (COPA), which restricted access by minors to any material deemed harmful to minors on the Internet. Both of these acts were overturned by courts because they violated constitutional rights to freedom of speech and the press.

In 2000 Congress passed the Children's Internet Protection Act of 2000 (CIPA). This act requires public libraries and K–12 schools that receive federal funds to take specific steps to protect minors from viewing harmful or obscene Internet content. These steps include adoption and implementation of an Internet safety policy that allows for monitoring the online activities of minors. The act also requires schools and libraries to install Internet filters or blocking software that prevents access to pictures that are obscene or harmful to minors. Adults using those computers can request to have the blocking software turned off. Many librarians oppose CIPA, asserting that blocking online information based on viewpoint or content violates the First Amendment. They contend that blocking software prevents access to certain works of art, music, health information, and other works representing different viewpoints, which are an important part of learning. Schools and libraries that do not receive federal funding are not required to comply with CIPA.

In addition to protecting children from indecent content, some legislation has been aimed at protecting children's privacy online. The Children's Online Privacy Protection Act (COPPA) was passed by Congress in 1998 and went into effect in 2000. COPPA was passed to address the rapid growth of online marketing that targeted children. Before COPPA, websites could collect personal data from children without their parents' knowledge or consent. The act restricts marketing to Internet users under the age of thirteen and protects their privacy by requiring parental consent for the collection or use of any personal information online. The act details what must be included in a website's privacy policy and

Legally Liable for Content

Some countries have introduced legislation that puts Internet intermediaries such as ISPs, webmasters, site hosting companies, or forum moderators legally at risk for content posted by users on their services and websites. To avoid legal trouble and punishment, some intermediaries are voluntarily taking down websites or deleting content and comments that could possibly be seen as objectionable. In China private companies have designated entire divisions that are responsible for monitoring the content on social media sites, search engines, and online forums. They have deleted tens of millions of messages each year, based on the reviewers' judgment and daily orders from the country's ruling Communist Party.

In Brazil, authorities arrested a senior Google executive in 2012 when he did not take down online videos that allegedly slandered a political candidate, a violation of Brazil's election law. The company argued that it should not be responsible for the contents of videos uploaded by users to YouTube, which Google owns. The executive was released shortly after his arrest after agreeing to appear in court at a later, undetermined date.

the responsibilities the website operator has to protect children's privacy and safety online.

Protecting Intellectual Property

In recent years the US government has pursued the unauthorized use of intellectual property on the Internet, which costs American industry money and jobs every year. Intellectual property includes anything that is a creation of the mind, such as music, literature, artistic works, discoveries and inventions, symbols, and designs. Intellectual property is usually protected by copyright law, which gives the creator of a work the right to determine its use and distribution and to be paid for the use of the work. For example, when a musician writes and records a song, both the musician and the record label hold a copyright to the song. Fans must purchase the song if they want it and must get special permissions if they plan to use it in certain ways.

The Internet, however, made it easy for users to download music and other types of intellectual property without paying for it. This use of works protected by copyright law without permission is called copyright infringement. In 1998 Congress signed the Digital Millennium Copyright Act (DMCA) into law, making it a crime to discuss and distribute technology that could be used to get around copyright protections on the Internet. The act also establishes a system for removing copyrighted works that are being used improperly and determines who is responsible when a copyright infringement occurs. For example, a video posted on YouTube may be taken offline because of copyright infringement on the Katy Perry song playing in the background.

Singer Katy Perry performs in Berlin in early 2015. Although the Internet makes it easy for users to download the work of musicians and other artists without paying for it, doing so violates copyright laws that protect the work from such use.

The Immigration and Customs Enforcement (ICE) division of the Department of Homeland Security has targeted websites that link to illegal copies of music and films and sites that sell counterfeit goods. In 2010 it launched Operation In Our Sites, an initiative targeting the sale of counterfeit merchandise on the Internet. In December 2013 ICE worked with several foreign law enforcement agencies and seized 706 domain names that were illegally selling counterfeit merchandise online to unsuspecting consumers. Once a domain name is seized, it falls under the custody of the government involved in the operation. Users attempting to visit these sites find a banner that notifies them of the seizure and informs them about the federal crime of willful copyright infringement.

Critics of the seizures say that they are too extreme and may violate First Amendment rights and due process, the idea that every person should be treated fairly under the law. They point to the case of a legitimate hip-hop music site called Dajaz1 that was wrongfully seized in November 2010 on the basis that the site linked to copyrighted songs without permission. After thirteen months ICE determined that the links did not actually infringe on copyrights and returned the domain to its owner. No civil or criminal charges were filed. In 2012 three members of Congress wrote a letter to Attorney General Eric Holder and Secretary of Homeland Security Janet Napolitano, expressing their concern that due process was being violated. In the letter the three state, "Our concern centers on your Department's methods, and the process given, when seizing the domain names of websites whose actions and content are presumed to be lawful, protected speech."[33] They referenced the Dajaz1 website case, saying that the ICE seizure ultimately proved to be unfounded.

Free Speech on the Internet

The US Constitution strongly protects free speech and freedom of the press. In 1997 the US Supreme Court ruled that Internet speech was protected under the Constitution, while lower courts have consistently struck down attempts to regulate online content. When someone uses the Internet to threaten or harass others, however, they cross a line. In 2010 Tara Elonis obtained a protective order against her estranged husband, Anthony, after he had posted several threatening comments on Facebook about her. About a week after she obtained the order Anthony posted on his Facebook page, "Fold up your PFA [protection-from-abuse order] and put it in your pocket. Is it thick enough to stop a bullet?" Anthony also posted threats to his coworkers at an amusement park in Allentown, Pennsylvania, and local elementary schools. In one post he wrote, "Enough elementary schools in a ten mile radius to initiate the most heinous school shooting ever imagined."[34] After his boss saw the postings, he called the FBI. Anthony was arrested, and a jury convicted him in 2011 on four counts of transmitting threatening communications in interstate commerce. He was sentenced to forty-four months in prison.

Anthony Elonis appealed his conviction, and his lawyers argued that his conviction violated his constitutional right to freedom of speech. Anthony claimed that he did not mean the threats he posted online. "I would never hurt my wife," he told the jury. "I never intended to threaten anyone."[35] He also argued that a person should not be convicted of making threats without proof that the speaker intended the speech to be a threat. "Internet users may give vent to emotions on which they have no intention of acting, memorializing expressions of momentary anger or exasperation that once were communicated face-to-face among friends and dissipated harmlessly,"[36] says a brief filed on Anthony's behalf by the Student Press Law Center, the Electronic Frontier Foundation, and the writers organization PEN.

Prosecutors argued that threats should be judged based on whether a reasonable person would have viewed the speech as a threat, and that the right to free speech does not give people the right to threaten and harass. According to a brief filed by the National Network to End Domestic Violence, victims "have experienced real-life terror caused by increasingly graphic and public posts to Facebook and other social media sites—terror that is exacerbated precisely because abusers now harness the power of technology, 'enabling them to reach their victims' everyday lives at the click of a mouse or the touch of a screen.'"[37]

In 2015 the US Supreme Court overturned Elonis's conviction. The justices ruled that it was not sufficient to convict Elonis based on the argument that a reasonable person would have seen his social media posts as threatening. Rather, the ruling stated, the posts had to be intended as threats for there to be a conviction. Steven Shapiro, national legal director of the American Civil Liberties Union, agreed with the Court's decision. He said that it properly required the legal system to prove criminal intent before convicting a person. He added that the use of the Internet did not change this basic legal requirement.

A Complex Issue

As the Internet continues to evolve with new users, technologies, and uses, the question of how to regulate the worldwide network and its millions of global users will only become more complex. How countries choose to address these issues, whether they view the Internet as a benefit or a threat, will have an impact on how people globally will be able to access and use the online world.

Chapter Five

Internet of the Future

Focus Questions

1. How do you envision the Internet of Things affecting your life?
2. Do you think it is ever justified to commercialize Internet access as a means to financing network expansion and upgrades? Why or why not?
3. What effect would Internet roadblocks set up by different countries have on overall Internet use? Do you see this as a problem? Why or why not?

"With the spread of connectivity and mobile phones around the world, citizens will have more power than at any other time in history, but it will come with costs, particularly to both privacy and security."

—Eric Schmidt, executive chairman of Google, and Jared Cohen, founder and director of Google Ideas.

Eric Schmidt and Jared Cohen, *The New Digital Age: Transforming Nations, Businesses, and Our Lives*. New York: Random House, 2014, p. 255.

The Internet has dramatically changed everyday life. It has created new ways to communicate and shop. It has become the go-to source for news and information for many people, while also opening new avenues for self-expression. And the Internet and World Wide Web are relatively young technologies that are still evolving. In the future the Internet may become even more seamlessly integrated into daily life, from the Internet-connected cars people drive to the data-collecting products they use. While this integration will bring many benefits and efficiencies, there are concerns about a further decrease of privacy and security.

In 2014 the Pew Research Center surveyed nearly fifteen hundred Internet experts and asked them about their predictions for the future of the Internet. Many of those surveyed agreed on several themes. Most respondents said that they believe the Internet would become like electricity in the next decade, effortless to access and important and embedded in everyday life. Joe Touch, director at the University of Southern California's Information Sciences Institute, predicts, "The Internet will shift from the place we find cat videos to a background capability that will be a seamless part of how we live our everyday lives. We won't think about 'going online' or 'looking on the Internet' for something—we'll just be online, and just look."[38] They also predicted that the Internet would become more mobile, wearable, and embedded into everyday objects, which will allow people to use, store, and share information no matter where they are or what they are doing.

Most experts also predicted that seamless connectivity to the Internet will enhance global connectivity, allowing people from different parts of the world to form relationships and foster understanding of each other. "It will be a world more integrated than ever before. We will see more planetary friendships, rivalries, romances, work teams, study groups, and collaborations,"[39] writes Bryan Alexander, senior fellow at the National Institute for Technology in Liberal Education.

Yet, while most of the experts surveyed agreed on how the Internet will evolve, they held differing opinions on the impact of the changes on society. "It is striking how much consensus there is among these experts on what will change, and equally striking how varied their answers are when they are asked how those changes will impact and influence users in good and bad ways,"[40] says Elon University professor Janna Anderson, a primary author of the Pew report.

The Internet of Things

As broadband Internet has become more widely available and the cost to go online has decreased, manufacturers are creating more devices with sensors and Internet capabilities. Most experts predict that the Internet will expand to encompass all of these devices and create an Internet of Things (IoT). Simply explained, the IoT is the idea of connecting many devices to the Internet and to each other. Everyday objects will be able to connect to online networks, through which they will be able to send and receive data. From cell phones to washing machines, the IoT will include a wide variety of connected devices. It also will include machine components such as the engine of a car or the drill on an oil rig. These objects

Experts predict that in the future, the Internet will expand to connect a much wider variety of devices than are normally connected today, such as a car engine or the drill on an oil rig like the one pictured here.

will have technology to monitor internal states and the external environment and then send this information where it needs to go online. If a device can be powered on and off, it will likely be part of the IoT. According to Gartner, an information technology research firm, there will be over 26 billion connected devices by 2020. Overall, experts say that the IoT connectivity will result in more data gathered from more devices and places, which will lead to increased efficiencies and improved safety and security.

Internet of Things (IoT)

The idea of connecting many devices to the Internet and each other.

The Internet of Things will have an effect on daily life in many ways. For example, to start the day, a connected alarm clock could wake up a person at 6:00 a.m. and then send a message to a coffeemaker to start brewing. On the way to a meeting, a person's car could connect to his or her online calendar to determine the location of the meeting and calculate the best route to take. If traffic causes a delay, the car could send a text to others attending the meeting so that they will know that the person is going to be late. At the office, printers, faxes, and other machines could monitor when they are running low on supplies and automatically reorder what is needed. Wearable devices can produce reports about where and when a person is most active and productive during the day.

The IoT may also be used by towns, cities, and countries to reduce waste, improve efficiencies, and maximize energy use. In some cities, programs have already been put in place to use the data provided by connected devices. In San Francisco, sensors detect which parking spaces are used and which are open. Drivers can use a mobile app to see real-time parking availability, which saves drivers time and gas and helps the city monitor pricing and supply. In Boston, the StreetBump app allows residents to report road conditions using their smartphones to detect bumps and potholes on their drive and then send the information to the city. "Isn't the responsibility of government to use resources like these inputs to make the smartest, most efficient decisions, as fast as possible?"[41] asks Brett Goldstein, a senior fellow in urban science at the University of Chicago Harris School of Public Policy.

A worker repairs a pothole on a Boston street. Residents of the city can use a smartphone app to report bumps and potholes in the streets, which officials hope will reduce the need for city workers to survey roadways to locate such problems.

The IoT will also create many opportunities for businesses. With objects and machines able to signal where they are and what they are doing, businesses will have new ways and information to improve operations and create new products. For example, in the chemical manufacturing industry, production equipment with sensors will enable companies to monitor the production process more closely. The sensors will send real-time data during the production process to computers, which will then analyze the data and send signals back to the machines that will immediately fine-tune production. The ability for these machines to communicate immediately will improve overall manufacturing efficiency as well as improve the quality of the products. "With objects that can signal where they are and what they're doing, companies have whole new ways to improve their operations,"[42] says Michael Chui, a principal at the McKinsey Global Institute.

Security and Privacy Concerns

While the IoT will bring new opportunities, it may also lead to new challenges. Security and privacy will become top concerns as more devices are connected to online networks, providing even more opportunities for privacy invasions and security breaches. Some people fear that sensors on everyday objects could be used by governments and others to track a person's movements and activities without his or her knowledge. "Risks to individual privacy and personal freedom could be sizeable," warns Chui. "The same video sensor and recognition technologies that can help find a heart attack victim in a crowded stadium could be used by a repressive government to detect where its political enemies are gathering."[43]

In 2014 several of the world's top data privacy commissioners met to discuss privacy risks associated with Internet-connected devices. "These devices can make our lives much easier," the data and privacy commissioners said in a declaration. "The internet of things however, can also reveal intimate details about the doings and goings of their owners through the sensors they contain. Personal development should not be defined by what business and government know about you. The proliferation of the internet of things increases the risk that this will happen."[44]

Privacy may be additionally compromised by the unauthorized sharing of personal data collected by manufacturers who make the countless objects connected in the Internet of Things. Manufacturers may find that they can profit from selling data to interested parties about how many steps a person takes in a day or whether food is running low in the kitchen. Many companies say that they do not sell individual data but instead sell only aggregated anonymous data, which is a large group of details about many people. Even so, privacy experts contend that this information has enough clues about individuals to make it possible for others to identify them.

The world's top data privacy commissioners take the position that companies who offer IoT devices should not collect personal data without the user's knowledge and consent. "Transparency is key: those who offer internet of things devices should be clear

Car Sharing

The IoT may lead to new ways of owning and using vehicles. Already, car-sharing sites like Wheelz and RelayRides offer an alternative to owning a car. Car owners post their cars to be rented by the hour or the day. Users search the sites to find a nearby car and put in a request to rent it. Once approved by the car's owner, the user drives off. This system of car sharing makes sure that cars are used as much as possible, not sitting idly.

Technology from the IoT may further increase the ease of car sharing. Many new cars already come with technology that allows them to be unlocked and started remotely from a mobile phone. Owners could open the car for a renter from anywhere. With more IoT technology, car-sharing services may become more popular as sensors and connections allow more detailed information to be tracked and shared with users. One day, a sensor may allow a shared car to "recognize" a driver as he or she approaches and unlocks the car. The sensors can then track where and how far the driver takes the car and where the driver leaves it for the next user.

about what data they collect, for what purposes and how long this data is retained,"[45] the privacy commissioners state. France's privacy commissioner, Isabelle Falque-Pierrotin, adds, "The Internet of things should stay under the control of the user."[46]

For device makers, however, the financial reward for selling personal data may be hard to ignore. Yale Zhang is a medical device entrepreneur based in Atlanta. His company, Safe Heart, makes a device called an iOximeter. It attaches to an individual's index finger and measures blood oxygen saturation, heart rate, and other information that is useful in medicine, sports, and aviation. The device can also collect data such as the location of the user, elevation, weather, and temperature. Currently, Zhang's device collects data and stores it locally on a user's smartphone for twenty-four hours. However, like many companies manufacturing IoT devices, Zhang faces a dilemma over what to do with his users' data. He says that data sharing can help patients, adding information to research pools for scientists to study. Data sharing can also be lucrative for his company. "If we were to sell the data, we could subsidize the cost of the device [for consumers], but how much is a single person's data worth?" he asks. "And if we do sell that information, and provide a discount, maybe we will, in response, have to ask identifying information such as gender, height, weight, age, so that the data that we provide to the data brokers or whoever is looking at this data will be worth more."[47] Zhang says that ideally, he would like to give his customers the choice of what happens to their data.

Challenges to the Open Internet

Since its inception the Internet has been free-flowing and open to most users. Yet concern is rising that the open Internet will be challenged in the future by practices that disrupt the way the Internet works. Several countries may choose increased blocking, filtering, and segmenting the Internet in an effort to maintain national security and political control. Some countries have already increased surveillance of Internet users. Countries such as Egypt, Pakistan, and Turkey have blocked Internet access in order to stop or control content that is perceived as a threat to existing leaders. The protests of the Arab Spring beginning in 2010 demonstrated the power of the Internet to organize political protest. Since then the trend of some governments' limiting information on the Internet has increased. Paul Saffo, managing director at equity research firm Discern Analytics, says, "The pressures to balkanize the global Internet will continue and create new uncertainties. Governments will become more skilled at blocking access to unwelcome sites."[48]

balkanize

To divide into smaller groups hostile to each other.

Fears about surveillance may also limit the free flow of information on the Internet. Governments concerned with surveillance and spying might set up roadblocks to geographically fragment the Internet, which will limit sharing and access to online information across borders. In 2013 Edward Snowden, an American computer professional, leaked thousands of classified documents that he had obtained while working as a contractor for the National Security Agency (NSA). The documents detailed several global surveillance programs, many run by the NSA, and included surveillance of e-mail, cloud-stored data, and other Internet sources. The surveillance revelations angered many citizens in the United States and countries around the world. A few months after the initial leaks Brazil announced plans to disconnect from the American Internet and technology companies. In 2014 the country began laying an undersea Internet cable to Europe to avoid American surveillance. Brazil also switched its main e-mail system from Microsoft Outlook to a state-developed system and required all government agencies to use state-owned companies for technology services. Fadi Chehadé is the president and chief executive of ICANN. He believes that international distrust over surveillance and privacy threaten the Internet. "I find myself in a unique point in history where either we will be able to succeed as a human race, almost, in maintaining the Internet as a platform for solidarity and for economic progress, or, frankly, we will fail," he says. "We

In 2013, former National Security Agency employee Edward Snowden (pictured) leaked classified documents that revealed the extent of the agency's surveillance of electronic data both domestic and foreign. The revelations sparked furious debate over issues relating to Internet privacy.

break it down, and politicize it, and fragment it to the point where it loses the incredible value it has in bringing us together."[49]

Net Neutrality

Another challenge to an open Internet is the pressure to commercialize, or charge money, for access. Over the years Internet traffic has increased significantly. Common practices such as video streaming and peer-to-peer file sharing require a substantial amount of bandwidth. Internet service providers have been forced to upgrade and expand their networks in order to handle increasing traffic loads. Some telecommunication

> **commercialize**
>
> To charge money in order to make a profit.

providers and technology companies believe that ISPs should be able charge a tiered fee structure, allowing companies to pay more to have their data sent faster than other Internet traffic. The added revenue would help pay for necessary network upgrades and expansions. Without the ability to recover some of their money, telecommunications companies may not be willing to build new broadband networks, which would limit available bandwidth and slow down the Internet.

Many people are opposed to the idea of charging more money for faster service online. They argue that net neutrality is a core component of the Internet. Net neutrality is the idea that Internet service providers should treat all data, websites, and services on the Internet in the same way. Those who support net neutrality believe that ISPs should not discriminate or charge different fees by user, content, site, platform, application, equipment, or communication method.

In November 2014 President Barack Obama voiced support for the preservation of net neutrality, calling on the FCC to regulate broadband Internet service like a utility such as water or electricity. In a statement released by the White House, Obama says, "We cannot allow Internet service providers (ISPs) to restrict the best access or to pick winners and losers in the online marketplace for services and ideas. I believe the FCC should create a new set of rules protecting net neutrality and ensuring that neither the cable company nor the phone company will be able to act as a gate-keeper, restricting what you can do or see online."[50] Obama also called for a ban on paid, fast access for content providers.

Industry groups that represent ISPs opposed President Obama's calls for net neutrality and plans for increased FCC regulation. David Cohen, executive vice president of telecommunications company Comcast Corp., says that Congress, not the White House, should decide if net neutrality rules are necessary. "The Internet has not just appeared by accident or gift—it has been built by companies like ours investing and building networks and infrastructure. The policy the White House is encouraging would

Divided Future

Some experts warn that the rising reliance on the Internet and data may lead to a new digital divide that creates an elite class of web and data-savvy users, causing those who are not as digitally connected to suffer. Pietro Ciminelli, the director of finance for BOCES (Boards of Cooperative Educational Services) in New York says that people who do not keep up their technical skills or are unwilling to accept the changing technology risk finding themselves unemployed, potentially increasing the divide between the wealthy and the poor.

Futurist Mike Osswald at Hanson, Inc., a digital strategy and marketing firm, warns that increasing reliance on the Internet may harm society as a whole:

> The rapid pace of technological change will only hurt the poor and lower-middle class (and third-world and mass-labor markets) who will not be able to benefit fully from the improvements, and will only continue to be displaced by technical/robotic solutions that limit their ability to earn a living and provide for their families. To this extent, technology will make society as a whole worse than in the past.

Quoted in Janna Anderson and Lee Rainie, "Digital Life in 2025," Pew Research Center, March 11, 2014. www.pewinternet.org.

jeopardize this engine for job creation and investment as well as the innovation cycle that the Internet has generated,"[51] he says.

In February 2015 the FCC voted to implement net neutrality rules that would require ISPs to treat all content equally. The new rules classify ISPs as public utilities, which makes them subject to FCC regulations that ensure all customers get fair access to services. Tiered fee structures under which ISPs could send data faster for companies who pay more are banned under the new rules. "The Internet is too important to allow broadband providers to make the rules," says FCC chairman Tom Wheeler. "So today after a decade of debate in an open, robust year-long process, we finally have legally sustainable rules to ensure that the Internet stays fast, fair and open."[52]

net neutrality

Treating all data, websites, and services on the Internet in the same way.

An Exciting Future

Since its introduction the Internet has changed, adapted, and integrated into many aspects of society. The Internet's impact on lives around the world has just begun, with many new technologies and uses in development. "As we look into the future—its promises and its challenges—we are facing a brave new world, the most fast-paced and exciting period in human history. We'll experience more change at a quicker rate than any previous generation, and this change, driven in part by the devices in our own hands, will be more personal and participatory than we can even imagine,"[53] write Eric Schmidt and Jared Cohen. While it may be impossible to predict the Internet of the future, it is certain that the road society will travel to reach it will be exciting.

Introduction: A Transformative Technology

1. Eric Schmidt and Jared Cohen, *The New Digital Age: Transforming Nations, Businesses, and Our Lives*. New York: Random House, 2014, p. 4.

2. James Manyika and Charles Roxburgh, "The Great Transformer: The Impact of the Internet on Economic Growth and Prosperity," McKinsey Global Institute, October 2011.

Chapter One: Connecting Computers Worldwide

3. Manuel Castells, "The Impact of the Internet on Society: A Global Perspective," *MIT Technology Review*, September 8, 2014. www.technologyreview.com.

4. Lee Rainie and Barry Wellman, *Networked: The New Social Operating System*. Cambridge, MA: MIT Press, 2012, p. 18.

5. Rainie and Wellman, *Networked: The New Social Operating System,* p. 80.

6. Schmidt and Cohen, *The New Digital Age*, p. 3.

Chapter Two: Opening the World and Sharing Online

7. Quoted in Seth Masket, "Don't Fear the Network: The Internet Is Changing the Way We Communicate for the Better," *PC Mag*, June 2, 2014.

8. Quoted in Rainie and Wellman, *Networked: The New Social Operating System,* p. 129.

9. Pamela Hartzband and Jerome Groopman, "Untangling the Web—Patients, Doctors, and the Internet," *New England Journal of Medicine*, March 25, 2010. www.nejm.org.

10. Quoted in Ellis Hamburger, "More than a Social Network: Facebook Aims to Be the Source for Breaking News," Verge, April 24, 2014. www.theverge.com.

11. Manyika and Roxburgh, "The Great Transformer."

12. Quoted in BGF, "How the Internet Changed the World," 2012. www.businessgrowthfund.co.uk.

13. Rainie and Wellman, *Networked: The New Social Operating System,* p. 255.

Chapter Three: Who Controls Information Online?

14. Nat Maple, "The Eternal Life of Your Data," Techradar, December 5, 2014. www.techradar.com.
15. Quoted in NDTV.com, "Survey Finds People Feel Loss of Control over Personal Information," November 13, 2014. http://gadgets.ndtv.com.
16. Schmidt and Cohen, *The New Digital Age,* p. 55.
17. Maple, "The Eternal Life of Your Data."
18. Quoted in Gartner, "Gartner Says That Consumers Will Store More than a Third of Their Digital Content in the Cloud by 2016," June 25, 2012. www.gartner.com.
19. Quoted in Melissa Riofrio, "The 5 Biggest Online Privacy Threats of 2013," *PC World*, April 8, 2013. www.pcworld.com.
20. Quoted in Riofrio, "The 5 Biggest Online Privacy Threats of 2013."
21. Quoted in Alan Duke, "5 Things to Know About the Celebrity Nude Photo Hacking Scandal," CNN.com, October 12, 2014. www.cnn.com.
22. Quoted in Duke, "5 Things to Know About the Celebrity Nude Photo Hacking Scandal."
23. Quoted in Riofrio, "The 5 Biggest Online Privacy Threats of 2013."
24. Quoted in Riofrio, "The 5 Biggest Online Privacy Threats of 2013."
25. Quoted in Riofrio, "The 5 Biggest Online Privacy Threats of 2013."
26. Quoted in Valarie Gonzalez, "Local Man Arrested After Stalking Woman Online," KGNS, August 15, 2014. www.kgns.tv.
27. Quoted in Tammie Sutherland, "U.S. Cyber Stalker Convicted After Being Duped by Toronto Dad," *City News*, December 5, 2014. www.citynews.ca.
28. Quoted in Sutherland, "U.S. Cyber Stalker Convicted After Being Duped by Toronto Dad."

29. Bruce Schneier, "The Internet Is a Surveillance State," CNN, March 16, 2013. www.cnn.com.
30. Quoted in Dan Tynan, "Our Internet Privacy Is at Risk—but Not Dead (Yet)," InfoWorld, April 22, 2013. www.infoworld.com.

Chapter Four: Regulating the Internet

31. Quoted in Freedom House, "New Report: Internet Freedom Deteriorates Worldwide, but Activists Push Back," October 3, 2013. https://freedomhouse.org.
32. Sanja Kelly et al., "Freedom on the Net 2013: A Global Assessment of Internet and Digital Media," Freedom House, October 3, 2013.
33. Quoted in Dara Kerr, "Homeland Security's Domain Seizures Worries Congress," CNET, September 3, 2012. www.cnet .com.
34. Quoted in Brent Kendall, "Supreme Court Agrees to Hear Internet Free-Speech Case," *Wall Street Journal*, June 16, 2014.
35. Quoted in Emily Bazelon, "Do Online Death Threats Count as Free Speech?," *New York Times*, November 25, 2014. www .nytimes.com.
36. Quoted in Robert Barnes, "Supreme Court Case Tests the Limits of Free Speech on Facebook and Other Social Media," *Washington Post*, November 23, 2014. www.washington post.com.
37. Quoted in Barnes, "Supreme Court Case Tests the Limits of Free Speech on Facebook and Other Social Media."

Chapter Five: Internet of the Future

38. Quoted in Janna Anderson and Lee Rainie, "Digital Life in 2025," Pew Research Center, March 11, 2014. www.pew internet.org.
39. Quoted in Anderson and Rainie, "Digital Life in 2025."
40. Quoted in Bridget Shirvell, "15 Predictions for the Future of the Internet," PBS.org, March 11, 2014. www.pbs.org.
41. Brett Goldstein, "When Government Joins the Internet of Things," *New York Times*, September 8, 2013. www.nytimes .com.

42. Michael Chui, "The Internet of Things Can Help Businesses to Do More, and Do It Better," *New York Times*, September 8, 2013. www.nytimes.com.
43. Chui, "The Internet of Things Can Help Businesses to Do More, and Do It Better."
44. Quoted in Adam Tanner, "World's Top Privacy Experts Worry About Internet of Things," *Forbes*, October 20, 2014. www.forbes.com.
45. Quoted in Tanner, "World's Top Privacy Experts Worry About Internet of Things."
46. Quoted in Tanner, "World's Top Privacy Experts Worry About Internet of Things."
47. Quoted in Adam Tanner, "Health Entrepreneur Debates Going to Data's Dark Side," *Forbes*, September 16, 2014. www.forbes.com.
48. Quoted in Janna Anderson and Lee Rainie, "Net Threats," Pew Research Center, July 3, 2014. www.pewinternet.org.
49. Quoted in Nancy Scola, "ICANN Chief: 'The Whole World Is Watching' the U.S.'s Net Neutrality Debate," *Washington Post*, October 7, 2014. www.washingtonpost.com.
50. Barack Obama, "Statement by the President on Net Neutrality," White House, November 10, 2014. www.whitehouse.gov.
51. Quoted in Mike Snider and Roger Yu, "Obama's Net Neutrality Push Cheers Some, Riles Others," *USA Today*, November 10, 2014. www.usatoday.com.
52. Quoted in Roger Yu and Mike Snider, "FCC Approves New Net Neutrality Rules," *USA Today*, February 26, 2015. www.usatoday.com.
53. Schmidt and Cohen, *The New Digital Age*, p.55.

Books

Cynthia A. Bily, *The Internet*. Farmington Hills, MI: Greenhaven, 2012.

danah boyd, *It's Complicated: The Social Lives of Networked Teens*. New Haven, CT: Yale University Press, 2014.

Ted Claypoole and Theresa Payton, *Protecting Your Internet Identity: Are You Naked Online?* Lanham, MD: Rowman & Littlefield, 2012.

Stephen Currie, *How Is the Internet Eroding Privacy Rights?* San Diego, CA: ReferencePoint, 2014.

Lee Rainie and Barry Wellman, *Networked: The New Social Operating System*. Cambridge, MA: MIT Press, 2012.

Eric Schmidt and Jared Cohen, *The New Digital Age: Transforming Nations, Businesses, and Our Lives*. New York: Random House, 2014.

Suzanne Weinick, *Understanding Your Rights in the Information Age*. New York: Rosen, 2013.

Internet Sources

Freedom House, "Freedom on the Net 2014: A Global Assessment of Internet and Digital Media," https://freedomhouse.org/report/freedom-net/freedom-net-2014.

Pew Research Center, "Digital Life in 2025," March 11, 2014. www.pewinternet.org/2014/03/11/digital-life-in-2025.

Pew Research Center's Internet & American Life Project, "Anonymity, Privacy, and Security Online," September 5, 2013. http://pewinternet.org/Reports/2013/Anonymity-online.aspx.

Pew Research Center's Internet & American Life Project, "Teens, Social Media, and Privacy," May 21, 2013. www.pewinternet.org/2013/05/21/teens-social-media-and-privacy.

Websites

GetNetWise (www.getnetwise.org). Information and tutorials about the latest issues and concerns facing Internet users, including safety, wireless security, and spyware.

NetSmartz (www.netsmartz.org). From the National Center for Missing and Exploited Children, this site has information about topics that relate to privacy and social media, including cyberbullying, revealing too much information, social networking, and more.

OnGuard Online (www.onguardonline.gov). This site provides practical tips from the federal government and the technology industry to help users be on guard against Internet fraud, secure their computers, and protect their personal information.

Privacy.org (www.privacy.org). This site offers the latest news, information, and initiatives on privacy. It is a joint project of the Electronic Privacy Information Center and Privacy International.

StaySafeOnline (www.staysafeonline.org). From the National Cyber Security Alliance, this site offers information and tools to help people use the Internet safely and securely at home, work, and school.

impact of, on modern life, 18–20
important dates in history of, **6–7**
origin of, 11–14
permanence of data on, 37
World Wide Web and, 14–16
See also regulation
Internet Architecture Board (IAB), 48
Internet Corporation for Assigned
    Names and Numbers (ICANN), 48
Internet Engineering Task Force (IETF),
    48
Internet of Things (IoT), 62–64
    definition of, 63
Internet Society, 48

Kelly, Sanja, 47, 50–51

Lawson, Gregor, 32
Listservs (automatic electronic mailing
    lists), 27
    definition of, 27
location data, 41–42
Lynch, Jennifer, 41–42

Manyika, James, 10, 31
Maple, Nat, 35, 37
Martin, Trayvon, 30
McKinsey Global Institute, 31
Middleton, Kate, **29**
Mitchell, Andy, 29
Mubarak, Hosni, 52–53

National Telecommunications and
    Information Administration (NTIA), 53
net neutrality, 69–71
    definition of, 71
network, definition of, 11
New Digital Age, The (Schmidt and
    Cohen), 8
news feeds, definition of, 28
Newswire (Facebook page), 29

Obama, Barack, 51, 69
Occupy movement, 30
Operation In Our Sites, 57
opinion polls. *See* surveys
Osswald, Mike, 70

packets, 20
Perry, Katie, 56, **56**
Pew Research Center, 61
Pew Research Center's Internet &
    American Life Project, 26
Pew Research Center's Project for
    Excellence in Journalism (PEJ), 28
Pew Research Internet Project, 17,
    18
polls. *See* surveys
privacy
    Internet of Things and, 65–67
    legislation on, 51
    personal, decrease in, 34–36
protocols, definition of, 12

Rainie, Lee, 18, 19, 33
regulation
    definition of, 50
    free speech and, 57–58
    in protection of intellectual property,
        55–57
    in protection of minors, 54–55
    restrictive, 50–53
    in United States, 53
Roxburgh, Charles, 10, 31

Saffo, Paul, 67
Schmidt, Eric, 8, 20, 37, 60, 71
Schneier, Bruce, 45–46
Scully, Bill, 37
search engines, 15–16
    definition of, 24
Simpson, John M., 39, 40
Skype (video-conference service), 9,
    22
Snowden, Edward, 67, **68**
social media/social networking sites,
    17, 22–23
    governments restricting, 52
    as news source, 28–30
Stanley, Jay, 41
Stauffer, Tim, 26
surveillance, government, 67–69
surveys
    on business use of web
        technologies, 31